Bonnie

This is just a small token of appreciation for your support and leadership in the Des Moines State. I look forward to working with you in the coming years. May the Lord bless you and your family as you serve in this important position.

Sincerely
Joe Chaney
98-99

HIS
HOLY
NAME

HIS HOLY NAME

DALLIN H. OAKS

BOOKCRAFT
SALT LAKE CITY, UTAH

Library of Congress Catalog Card Number 98-68061
ISBN 1-57008-592-7

First Printing, 1998

Printed in the United States of America

CONTENTS

Contents

PREFACE

This book is about the name of Jesus Christ. His holy name is "above every name" (Philip. 2:9). It is woven through the fabric of our religious life—through all of the eternally important things the children of God experience upon this earth. His holy name is invoked in prayer, in baptism, in sacred covenants (such as marriage), and in the blessings of the holy temples.

When I was called as an Apostle I went to the scriptures for illumination on my responsibilities. I found that I was called to be one of the "special witnesses of the name of Christ in all the world" (D&C 107:23). A witness of Christ I could understand, but why a witness of the *name of Christ?*

Sensitized by this unanswered question, I have been amazed at how often scriptural teachings on very important subjects refer to the name of Jesus Christ rather than to the Savior Himself. There is something important here— something heretofore rarely discussed in our literature.

This book is the product of more than a decade of prayerful study and pondering on the meaning and significance of scriptural references to the holy name of Jesus Christ. With illumination from the Holy Spirit, it has grown "line upon line, precept upon precept" (D&C 98:12), but even now it only scratches the surface of a subject that is deep and important.

I have been helped by many associates whom I have provoked to discussions on the matters treated in this book. I thank all of them for their valuable assistance. On chapter 5 I have benefited from the research and insights of Professors Joseph Fielding McConkie and H. Curtis Wright. I am indebted to my secretary, Dixie Derrick, for her untiring processing of an evolving manuscript. We mourned her sudden death just after the manuscript was completed. Finally, and most of all, I express profound gratitude to my dear wife, June, for her stalwart support and patience as she battled cancer during the last year of this book's preparation. She participated in my joy when it was accepted for publication, and died two weeks later.

This is not an easy book, nor is it a definitive one. It is not easy because it deals with ideas that are complex and difficult to explain, especially when applied to a multitude of scriptural texts. It is not definitive because it does not purport to declare the doctrine of The Church of Jesus Christ of Latter-day Saints or even to give any official Church position on the meaning of any particular scripture. Only the President of the Church or the First Presidency can perform those sacred functions. Modern revelation clearly declares that an Apostle can write "by wisdom," but not by commandment (D&C 28:5).

What is written here is a personal expression that attempts to offer wisdom on the meaning of a frequent and important reference in our scriptures, ancient and modern. I pray that the thoughts written here will achieve their intended purpose to motivate and illuminate their readers' studies of the gospel of Jesus Christ as revealed in the holy scriptures and in other teachings and testimonies inspired by the Holy Ghost.

Chapter 1

USES OF NAME

*T*he word *name* occurs in the scriptures about 1500 times, mostly as references to Deity or to the name of Deity.

Instead of directly referring to God the Father or to His Son, Jesus Christ, many passages of scripture refer to "the name of the Lord," to "his name," or to "my name." Thus, the scriptures describe praying as calling upon the name of the Lord (e.g., Gen. 4:26; D&C 65:4). They teach that miracles are done by the power of His name (see Acts 4:10; 3 Ne. 8:1). They state that temples are built to His name (e.g., 1 Chr. 22:19; D&C 109:78). They declare that salvation and the remission of sins come through His name or to those who believe on His name (e.g., Acts 10:43; Alma 5:48). And they declare that there is no other name given whereby man can be saved (e.g., Acts 4:12; Mosiah 3:17).

Scores of scriptures proclaim praise to His name or pronounce His name blessed (e.g., Ps. 135:1; Matt. 21:9). Apostles are called to be special witnesses of His name in

1

all the world (see D&C 107:23). The Seventies Quorum is instituted for traveling elders to bear record of His name in all the world (see D&C 124:139). Men are called to proclaim His name, to bear His name, or to suffer for His name (e.g., Acts 9:15–16; D&C 112). In partaking of the sacrament, members of His Church covenant that they are willing to take His name upon them (see D&C 20:77). (All of the scriptures cited here and many others of similar meaning are discussed hereafter.)

Scriptures referring to names other than the name of Deity further illustrate the importance of a name. Genesis reports Adam's giving every living creature a name (see Gen. 2:19). The Lord specified the name to be given or a changed name to be taken by some of the most prominent persons in the Bible (e.g., Abraham, Gen. 17:5; John the Baptist, Luke 1:13, 60–63). As a token of their diligence in keeping God's commandments, the prophet/king Benjamin gave his people a new name (see Mosiah 1:11). The names "Nephites" and "Lamanites," so familiar in the Book of Mormon, are often explained in that book as what a particular people were "called" because of their religious commitment or political allegiance, rather than as a description of their lineage (e.g., Jacob 1:14; Alma 3:10–11; 4 Ne. 1:36, 38).

If names are so important for mortals, how much more important is the name of God! Our earliest scriptures affirm such importance in the divine commandment, "Thou shalt not take the name of the Lord thy God in vain" (Ex. 20:7), and in the fact that under the Mosaic law the penalty for blaspheming the name of the Lord was death by stoning (see Lev. 24:16).

What is the meaning and significance of the word *name* when it refers to Deity? The many different usages of *name* in the scriptures suggest that there is more than one meaning. This book will explore some of those meanings.

Chapter 2 reviews the scriptural use of "name" in its most familiar meaning—to identify the person named. Chapter 3 examines instances where the name of God means the authority or priesthood or power of God. Chapter 4 discusses many different scriptures where the "name" of God seems to mean the work or plan of God. Chapter 5 brings different meanings together in its review of scriptures in which the "name" of God seems to signify His essence or the subject of exaltation. Finally, chapter 6 applies all of these meanings to three important groups of scriptures referring to the name of the Lord: the sacrament covenant that we are willing to take His name upon us, the Apostle's duty to be a witness of His name, and the significance of belief in Christ in contrast to belief in His name.

Chapter 2

NAME AS IDENTIFICATION

*J*esus taught us to pray: "Our Father which art in heaven, Hallowed be thy name" (Matt. 6:9; 3 Ne. 13:9). Surely no names evoke more reverence among the devout than the holy names of God the Father and His Son Jesus Christ. Reverence for the Holy Being includes reverence for His holy name.

The first dictionary meaning of the word *name* is a word or words by which a person is identified, designated, or known. Consequently, a scriptural reference to the "name" of the Father or the Son can be simply a reference to God Himself. Thus, one early dictionary of the Bible states that in many usages in the New Testament "the name of Jesus is a parallel term to the word 'Jesus' itself" (*Dictionary of the Bible* [James Hastings, ed., New York: Charles Scribner's Sons, 1900], 3:480). It is probably not an overstatement to say that this meaning, identification, is the meaning most readers assume for most scriptural references to the name of Deity.

When *name* is used as or to signify identification, to

call upon the name of God or to give thanks to the name of God means to call upon or give thanks to God Himself. In this usage the word *name* is used interchangeably with the Being named. Many verses or passages of scripture seem to illustrate this usage. (For ease of reference, the key words relating to "name" are reproduced here in boldface.) Examples include:

And in that day Adam **blessed God** and was filled, and began to prophesy concerning all the families of the earth, saying: **Blessed be the name of God.** [Moses 5:10]

O give thanks unto the LORD; . . .
And say ye, Save us, **O God of our salvation,** . . . that we may **give thanks to thy holy name,** [and] glory in thy praise. [1 Chr. 16:34–35]

Praise the LORD, call upon his name, declare his doings among the people, make mention that **his name is exalted.** [Isa. 12:4; see also 2 Ne. 22:4]

He that **believeth on him** is not condemned: but he that believeth not is condemned already, because he hath not **believed in the name** of the only begotten Son of God. [John 3:18]

Pray unto the Lord, call upon his holy name, make known his wonderful works among the people. [D&C 65:4]

In all of these examples the word *name* seems to be simply a synonym for God or the Lord Himself.

To cite another example, in his great sermon on Christ, King Benjamin frequently alternates between references to God or Christ (e.g., Mosiah 2:20, 28; 3:12; 4:2–3, 9; 5:5) and references to **"his name"** or the **"name of Christ"** or the **"name of the Lord"** (e.g., Mosiah 3:9, 17, 21; 4:11; 5:7). All or most of these references seem to have the same meaning. Other Book of Mormon passages using this same interchangeability, where *name* can be understood as simply a reference to the person named, are:

> There is **none other name given under heaven save it be this Jesus Christ,** of which I have spoken, whereby man can be saved. [2 Ne. 25:20]

> And they began from that time forth **to call on his name; therefore God conversed with men** and made known unto them the plan of redemption. [Alma 12:30]

> Now if this is boasting, even so will I boast. . . . Yea, **blessed is the name of my God,** who has been mindful of this people. [Alma 26:36]

> And behold, we are again delivered out of the hands of our enemies. And **blessed is the name of our God; for behold, it is he that has delivered us.** [Alma 57:35]

A clear usage of the word *name* to identify the person named is in the Savior's warning against deception in the last days: "For many shall **come in my name, saying, I am Christ;** and shall deceive many" (Matt. 24:5). Here the words *come in my name* are used to signify a person's identifying himself as Christ.

In other scriptures it is the context of the reference to the name of the Lord rather than grammatical interchangeability that suggests the meaning to be a direct reference to the Lord Himself. Following are examples:

And call ye on the name of your gods, and **I will call on the name of the LORD: and the God that answereth by fire, let him be God.** [1 Kings 18:24]

Behold, my beloved brethren, **remember the words of your God; pray unto him continually by day, and give thanks unto his holy name** by night. [2 Ne. 9:52]

In each of these references, the word *name* seems to be equivalent to a reference to God or the Lord Himself. Here "name" is used in its most familiar meaning, to identify or stand for the Being named.

Chapter 3

NAME AS AUTHORITY
OR PRIESTHOOD
OR POWER

*M*any scriptural references to the "name" of Jesus Christ seem to be references to the *authority* or *priesthood* or *power* of Jesus Christ. Some verses of scripture specifically define "name" in this manner. The clearest of these is the Lord's word to Abraham:

> Behold, I will lead thee by my hand, and I will take thee, **to put upon thee my name, even the Priesthood of thy father, and my power shall be over thee.** [Abr. 1:18.]

Similarly, Jesus appointed seventy and sent them out to preach and heal. Later, the scripture records: "And the seventy returned again with joy, saying, Lord, **even the devils are subject unto us through thy name**" (Luke 10:17).

The prescribed pattern of performing priesthood ordinances is to do them "in the name of Jesus Christ." In the earliest scriptural account of this, after Adam is taught the significance of the sacrifices he has been offering, he is commanded:

> Wherefore, thou shalt **do all that thou doest in the name of the Son,** and thou shalt repent and **call upon God in the name of the Son** forevermore. [Moses 5:8]

We have record that Moses followed this pattern in commanding Satan to depart:

> And now Satan began to tremble, and the earth shook; and Moses received strength, and called upon God, saying: **In the name of the Only Begotten, depart hence, Satan.** [Moses 1:21]

Similarly, the Book of Mormon prophet, Nephi, "**[did] many more miracles, in the sight of the people, in the name of Jesus**" (3 Ne. 7:20). In each of these scriptural references the name of the Lord signifies the priesthood authority or power of the Lord. These are all examples of how the power of God is invoked by the authorized use of His name.

The descriptions of Peter's miraculous healing of the lame man in the temple give greater detail on the usage of the word *name* both to mean priesthood authority and to invoke that authority. Peter declared, "**In the name of**

Jesus Christ of Nazareth rise up and walk" (Acts 3:6). After the man had been instantly healed, Peter explained to the multitude: "And **his name through faith in his name** hath made this man strong, whom ye see and know" (Acts 3:16). Later, when Peter and John were arrested and brought before the council for this action, they were asked: **"By what power, or by what name, have ye done this?"** (Acts 4:7.) Peter replied, **"By the name of Jesus Christ of Nazareth** . . . doth this man stand here before you whole" (Acts 4:10). The Saints then praised the Lord, "that **signs and wonders may be done by the name of the holy child Jesus"** (Acts 4:30).

Scores of scriptures record persons speaking or acting in the "name" of Jesus or the Lord, meaning by His authority. The words of the shepherd boy, David, are a well-known example. Clothed with the authority of his earlier anointing by the prophet Samuel (see 1 Sam. 16:13), David began his battlefield confrontation with the giant Goliath by declaring:

> Thou comest to me with a sword, and with a spear, and with a shield: but **I come to thee in the name of the LORD of hosts,** the God of the armies of Israel, whom thou hast defied. [1 Sam. 17:45]

A prominent Bible dictionary observes, "The prophets spoke in the name of the Lord—i.e., with divine authority (James 5:10)" (*The Interpreter's Dictionary of the Bible* [New York: Abingdon Press, 1962], 3:506). Ancient scriptures command that all things should be done in His name (see

Col. 3:17; 3 Ne. 27:7). Similarly, in modern revelation we are taught that what we ask "in the spirit" (meaning as directed by the Spirit) is asked "according to the will of God; wherefore it is done even as [we ask]" (D&C 46:30), but this promise is then conditioned on our acting in the prescribed way:

> And again, I say unto you, **all things must be done in the name of Christ,** whatsoever you do in the Spirit. [D&C 46:31]

The fact that we are commanded to do all things in the name of Christ does not mean that every use of His name signifies an act done by the power of His priesthood. An unauthorized person may use His holy name without authority in a purported ordinance. The prescribed baptismal prayer clearly illustrates the fact that one who performs a priesthood ordinance in the name of Jesus Christ must have been given authority to do so.

> *The person who is called of God and has authority from Jesus Christ to baptize,* shall go down into the water with the person . . . and shall say, . . . *Having been commissioned of Jesus Christ, I baptize you in the name of the Father, and of the Son, and of the Holy Ghost.* Amen. [D&C 20:73] [Emphasis added.]

In another revelation the Prophet Joseph Smith uses these same words to explain that in order to be efficacious, acts done in the name of the Lord must be done "in authority":

In all ages of the world, whenever the Lord has given a dispensation of the priesthood to any man by actual revelation, or any set of men, this power has always been given. Hence, *whatsoever those men did in authority, in the name of the Lord,* and did it truly and faithfully, and kept a proper and faithful record of the same, it became a law on earth and in heaven, and could not be annulled, according to the decrees of the great Jehovah. [D&C 128:9] [Emphasis added.]

The revelation on marriage teaches and applies this doctrine on a most important subject. After declaring that the covenants of eternal marriage must be administered by one whom the Lord has appointed to hold and exercise this power, the Lord declares:

Will I accept of an offering, saith the Lord, that is not made in my name?

Or will I receive at your hands that which I have not appointed? [D&C 132:9–10]

This truth is further stressed by the fact that one meaning of the commandment not to take the name of the Lord in vain (see Ex. 20:7) is not to use that holy name without authority. (See D&C 63:62, quoted at the end of this chapter.)

There are many other usages of the word *name* to signify priesthood authority. The revelation declaring that the Twelve are **"to officiate in the name of the Lord,** under the direction of the First Presidency of the Church, . . . to build up the Church and regulate all the affairs of the same in all nations" (D&C 107:33), clearly means that the Twelve are to "officiate in the [authority] of the Lord."

Another revelation describes those who come forth in the resurrection of the just as those "who received the testimony of Jesus, and **believed on his name**" (D&C 76:51). The words *believed on his name* can have several different meanings, but here the context suggests that they refer to believing in His priesthood and its ordinances. Thus, the persons who "believed on his name" are here described as "they who . . . were baptized" (v. 51) that "they might . . . receive the Holy Spirit by the laying on of the hands of him who is ordained and sealed unto this power" (v. 52). They are also described as those who were "sealed by the Holy Spirit of promise" (v. 53), and as "they who are priests and kings, who have received of his fulness" (v. 56) and are "priests of the Most High, after the order of Melchizedek" (v. 57).

Another illustration of *name* used to mean priesthood authority or power occurs in the two revelations concerning the dedication of the Kirtland Temple. In the Prophet Joseph Smith's dedicatory prayer he asked the Lord to "accept the dedication of this house . . . and also this church, to **put upon it thy name**" (D&C 109:78–79). When this prayer was offered, the Lord had already put His name upon the Church in the sense that the Church was identified by His name (see D&C 20:1; see also 115:4). What was prayed for in Kirtland must have been something more. What the Prophet prayed for was probably an endowment of authority or power for the temple work and

the Church. This interpretation was confirmed in the revelation of a week later, where the Lord accepted the Kirtland Temple and stated, "For behold, I have accepted this
house, and **my name shall be here**" (D&C 110:7). (Similarly, in accepting Solomon's Temple, the Lord said he
would **"put my name there"** [1 Kings 9:3].)

The meaning of the Lord's statement that His name
would be in the Kirtland Temple is suggested by the immediately succeeding appearance of the prophets Moses,
Elias, and Elijah, who conferred priesthood keys upon the
Prophet. In other words, when the Lord declared that His
name would be in the Kirtland Temple, He immediately
showed at least one meaning of that declaration by having
His delegated servants confer the priesthood keys under
which His authority would be exercised there (see D&C
110:12–16). The Prophet's prayer for the Lord to put His
name upon the Church was also answered in the conferral
of priesthood keys pertaining to the gathering of Israel
(see D&C 110:11).

In the foregoing examples and in many similar references in the scriptures, "name of the Lord" means or
seems to mean the "priesthood" or "power" of the Lord.

There are other scriptures in which "name" seems to
signify authority in the broader sense of an authorized
representative.

Dictionaries note that when one person acts in the
"name" of another, he acts as the deputy or representative
of the other or in behalf of the other. A Bible dictionary
describes this usage as follows: "To speak or act in some-
one's name is to act as the representative of that person

15

and hence to participate in his authority" (*Interpreter's Dictionary*, 3:502).

The scriptures have numerous illustrations of this usage (e.g., 1 Sam. 25:5, 9). The most elevated of these examples is when the Savior speaks for the Father in the first person as if He were the Father. This has been called "divine investiture of authority." President Joseph F. Smith and his counselors, in their 1916 doctrinal exposition titled "The Father and the Son," describe the basis for this:

> He declared . . . **"I am come in my Father's name"** (John 5:43; see also 10:25). . . . Thus the Father placed His name upon the Son; and Jesus Christ spoke and ministered in and through the Father's name; and so far as power, authority, and Godship are concerned His words and acts were and are those of the Father. [*Messages of the First Presidency*, 5:32 (James R. Clark, ed., Salt Lake City: Bookcraft, 1971), also in *Encyclopedia of Mormonism*, 4:1675]

The scriptures contain many examples of this divine investiture of authority, perhaps the most vivid being Doctrine and Covenants section 29, where Jesus Christ introduces Himself in verse 1 and then, in verse 42, speaks in the first person as the Father.

The scriptures also contain instances where individuals other than the Father or the Son have acted or spoken in the first person as Deity, by divine investiture of authority. Thus, the Lord sent an angel to guide Israel during the Exodus, and commanded them to "obey his voice, . . . **for** my name is in him" (Ex. 23:21). Similarly, the angel who visited the Apostle John spoke in the first person as if he were the Lord (e.g., Rev. 22:12–13, 16), but would not allow John to worship him, because, the angel declared, he was not the Lord (vv. 8–9).

In the familiar circumstance discussed earlier, in which we perform priesthood ordinances in our own identity but in behalf of the Lord ("in his name"), we act as His agents and by His authority. The Lord Himself used this familiar concept in a revelation given to guide the early leaders of His restored Church.

> Wherefore, as ye are agents, ye are on the Lord's errand; and whatever ye do according to the will of the Lord is the Lord's business. [D&C 64:29]

The efficacy of things that are done by an authorized agent in behalf of the Divine Master is affirmed in these revelations:

> Whether by mine own voice or by the voice of my servants, it is the same. [D&C 1:38]

> And I will lay my hand upon you by the hand of my servant Sidney Rigdon, and you shall receive my Spirit, the Holy Ghost, even the Comforter, which shall teach you the peaceable things of the kingdom. [D&C 36:2]

To perform ordinances in the authority of the priesthood is the most familiar illustration of acting as an agent of the Lord, but there are other examples of divine agency ("in the name of the Lord") not involving a direct exercise of priesthood authority. Unordained persons who teach the gospel are one example. Other examples include persons who act in the name of the Lord and further His work by praying or bearing testimony.

Of course, all must remember that one who assumes to use the name of the Lord—with or without priesthood authority—will be accountable for his or her use of that sacred representation:

> Wherefore, **let all men beware how they take my name in their lips**—
>
> For behold, verily I say, that **many there be who are under this condemnation, who use the name of the Lord, and use it in vain, having not authority.** . . .
>
> Remember that that which cometh from above is sacred, and must be spoken with care, and by constraint of the Spirit. [D&C 63:61–62, 64]

This caution applies to all that is done in the name of the Lord, from the performance of sacred priesthood ordinances at one end of the spectrum to the things said in sermons, teachings, and prayers at the other.

Chapter 4

NAME AS WORK
OR PLAN

*A*lthough there are various other vitally important meanings, the most frequent single meaning of the scriptures that refer to the name of the Lord seems to be *work of the Lord* (or *His work* or *My work*). For this purpose, "work of the Lord" includes the entirety of God's gospel plan for the salvation and exaltation of His children, most notably the Resurrection and Atonement of the Lord Jesus Christ. As the Lord God explained to Moses, "For behold, this is my work and my glory—to bring to pass the immortality and eternal life of man" (Moses 1:39).

Elder Neal A. Maxwell addressed this meaning in discussing an Apostle's scriptural duty to be a special witness of the name of Christ.

> To witness for the name of Jesus Christ is to witness of the reality of His having been anointed as

Lord and Savior; to witness of His deeds, especially His atonement; to witness of His attributes; and to witness of the Father's plan of salvation—in which Jesus is the redeeming centerpiece. [*If Thou Endure It Well* (Salt Lake City: Bookcraft, 1996), 106]

(The Apostle's duty is discussed in chapter 6 herein.)

To those blessed with the illumination of the restored gospel, the *priesthood* or *authority* meaning discussed in chapter 3 and the *work* or *plan* meaning discussed in this chapter are basically the same reality viewed from two different perspectives. To act in the authority of God is to do the work of God; to do the work of God we should have the authority of God.

The Book of Mormon records an impressive illustration of the importance of the meaning of *name* discussed in this chapter. It illustrates the use of "name" to identify the Lord's Church and then declares that something more is required. That something more is the *work* or *plan* meaning discussed here.

During the risen Lord's appearance to the Nephites on the American continent, they asked Him to settle a dispute by telling them "the name whereby we shall call this church" (3 Ne. 27:3). Jesus responded that the answer was to be found in the scriptures teaching that "ye must take upon you the name of Christ . . . for by this name shall ye be called at the last day" (v. 5). "Therefore," Jesus directed, "ye shall call the church in my name" (v. 7). Then the Savior gave an unusually detailed explanation of His answer. He began by illustrating the essential use of His "name" as a matter of identification. Then He explained that such name identification was not enough—the Church had to be built upon His gospel.

> And how be it my church save it be called in my name? For if a church be called in Moses' name then it be Moses' church; or if it be called in the name of a man then it be the church of a man; but *if it be called in my name then it is my church, if it so be that they are built upon my gospel.*
>
> Verily I say unto you, that *ye are built upon my gospel;* therefore ye shall call whatsoever things ye do call, in my name; therefore if ye call upon the Father, for the church, if it be in my name the Father will hear you;
>
> And *if it so be that the church is built upon my gospel* then will the Father show forth his own works in it.
>
> But *if it be not built upon my gospel, and is built upon the works of men, or upon the works of the devil,* verily I say unto you they have joy in their works for a season, and by and by the end cometh, and they are hewn down and cast into the fire, from whence there is no return. [3 Ne. 27:8–11] [Emphasis added.]

Succeeding verses give additional explanation of the meaning of being "built upon [His] gospel," which seems to be equivalent to "His work" or "His plan."

The rest of this chapter will give various important illustrations of this most common scriptural usage, in which "the name of Jesus Christ" or "His name" or "My name" means His work or His plan. We begin with references to the most fundamental part of that work or plan—the Atonement of Jesus Christ.

Forgiveness of Sins Comes Through His Name or Through Belief on His Name

Many scriptures declare that sins are forgiven through the name of Christ, or that He has suffered for the sins of those who believe on His name. In all of these scriptures, "name" seems to mean the Savior's great work of atonement and redemption.

To him give all the prophets witness, that **through his name whosoever believeth in him shall receive remission of sins.** [Acts 10:43]

And behold, it is he that cometh **to take away the sins of the world,** yea, **the sins of every man who steadfastly believeth on his name.** [Alma 5:48]

And he shall come into the world to redeem his people; and he shall **take upon him the transgressions of those who believe on his name;** and these are they that shall have eternal life, and salvation cometh to none else. [Alma 11:40]

And behold, he said unto them: Behold, I give unto you a sign; for five years more cometh, and behold, then cometh the Son of God **to redeem all those who shall believe on his name.** [Hel. 14:2]

I am Jesus Christ, the Son of God, who was **crucified for the sins of the world, even as many as will believe on my name,** that they may become the sons of God. [D&C 35:2]

As we know from many other teachings of the gospel, we need to do more than "believe in Christ" (see chapter 6). When we understand "His name" as being "His work" or "His plan," these scriptures teach that we must believe in the "work" or "plan" of Jesus Christ, including His atonement. Those who have this belief will act upon it by repenting, receiving His ordinances, and keeping His commandments. The Book of Mormon teaches this with clarity:

And **if ye believe on his name ye will repent of all your sins,** that thereby ye may have a remission of them through his merits. [Hel. 14:13]

SALVATION COMES THROUGH HIS NAME

Speaking more generally (about "salvation" rather than just about remission of sins), some scriptures teach that salvation comes through the name of Christ, declaring that there is no other name by which we are saved. For example, an important New Testament verse declares, "Neither is there salvation in any other: for there is **none other name under heaven given among men, whereby we must be saved"** (Acts 4:12). In such teachings, the word *name* seems to reference the entire gospel plan, including the Lord's atoning sacrifice pursuant to it. Some Book of Mormon scriptures even couple their use of "no other name" with the emphasizing words *none other way* or *no other . . . way nor means.*

> And now, behold, my beloved brethren, this is the way; and **there is none other way nor name given under heaven whereby man can be saved** in the kingdom of God. And now, behold, this is the doctrine of Christ. [2 Ne. 31:21]

> And moreover, I say unto you, that there shall be **no other name given nor any other way nor means whereby salvation can come** unto the children of men, **only in and through the name of Christ,** the Lord Omnipotent. [Mosiah 3:17]

WE MUST HAVE FAITH IN OR BELIEVE ON HIS NAME TO BE SAVED

In a variation of the teachings just discussed, other scriptures teach that men must have *faith in* or *believe on* the name of Jesus Christ in order to be "saved." None of these teachings can be understood without understanding the meaning of "saved" or "salvation." For this purpose it must mean being saved or having salvation in the celestial kingdom (for which baptism is a requirement) or being exalted to eternal life (for which the making and keeping of temple covenants are requirements). (See, generally, Dallin H. Oaks, "Have You Been Saved?," *Ensign,* May 1998, 55.)

The significance of faith or belief on His name in order to be saved or exalted is that we must have faith in and comply with His plan, including its requirements for ordinances and covenants and faithfulness to the end. This interpretation is confirmed by a Bible teaching that explains what it means to believe in the name of the Son.

> He that believeth on him is not condemned: **but he that believeth not is condemned already, because he hath not believed in the name of the only begotten Son of God;** *which before was preached by the mouth of the holy prophets; for they testified of me.* [John 3:18; italicized words added in JST]

After speaking these words, Jesus explained that "the condemnation" was that men did evil and did not come to the light (see vv. 19–20), whereas "he that doeth truth cometh to the light" (v. 21). In other words, he that "believed in the name" (v. 18) believed in the gospel of Jesus Christ (His work) and acted upon that belief in order to be saved.

Following are some of the other important scriptures declaring that we must have faith in or believe on His name to be saved.

And thus **he shall bring salvation to all those who shall believe on his name.** [Alma 34:15]

Yea, thus we see that **the gate of heaven is open unto all, even to those who will believe on the name of Jesus Christ,** who is the Son of God. [Hel. 3:28]

Behold, I am he who was prepared from the foundation of the world to redeem my people. Behold, I am Jesus Christ. I am the Father and the Son. **In me shall all mankind have life, and that eternally, even they who shall believe on my name;** and they shall become my sons and my daughters. [Ether 3:14]

For **no man can be saved,** according to the words of Christ, **save they shall have faith in his name.** [Moro. 7:38]

And we know that **all men must repent and believe on the name of Jesus Christ,** and worship the Father in his name, **and endure in faith on his name to the end, or they cannot be saved in the kingdom of God.** [D&C 20:29]

I came unto mine own, and mine own received me not; but unto as many as received me gave I power to do many miracles, and to become the sons of God; **and even unto them that believed on my name gave I power to obtain eternal life.** [D&C 45:8]

The several types of references discussed in the first part of this chapter illustrate the use of "His name" in describing the most fundamental concepts of the gospel of Jesus Christ: forgiveness of sins through His name (or belief on His name), salvation through His name, and faith on His name to be saved. These ideas are so central to the gospel that they are probably what is referred to when the Old Testament prophet declared, in words later quoted in the Lord's personal teachings in the New World:

> Then they that feared the LORD spake often one to another: and the LORD hearkened, and heard [it], and a book of remembrance was written before him **for them that feared the LORD, and that thought upon his name.**
>
> And they shall be mine, saith the LORD of hosts, in that day when I make up my jewels; and I will spare them, as a man spareth his own son that serveth him. [Mal. 3:16–17; see also 3 Ne. 24:16–17]

A TEMPLE IS BUILT TO HIS NAME

In the Old Testament and in modern scriptures, one of the most common descriptions of temples is that they are built to His name. This seems to mean that temples are built to carry out the work or plan of the Lord, including the sacred ordinances and covenants that open the door to salvation for the dead and to exaltation for the living and the dead.

David also commanded all the princes of Israel to help Solomon his son, [saying],

Now set your heart and your soul to seek the LORD your God; arise therefore, and build ye the sanctuary of the LORD God, to bring the ark of the covenant of the LORD, and the holy vessels of God, into **the house that is to be built to the name of the LORD.** [1 Chr. 22:17, 19]

I purpose to build an house unto the name of the LORD my God, as the LORD spake unto David my father. [1 Kings 5:5]

And the LORD hath performed his word that he spake, and I am risen up in the room of David my father, and sit on the throne of Israel, as the LORD promised, and **have built an house for the name of the LORD God of Israel.** [1 Kings 8:20]

Verily I say unto you, it is expedient in me that the first elders of my church should **receive their endowment from on high in my house, which I have commanded to be built unto my name** in the land of Kirtland. [D&C 105:33]

For thou knowest that we have done this work through great tribulation; and out of our poverty **we have given of our substance to build a house to thy name,** that the Son of Man might have a place to manifest himself to his people. [D&C 109:5]

O hear, O hear, O hear us, O Lord! And answer these petitions, and **accept the dedication of this house unto thee, the work of our hands, which we have built unto thy name.** [D&C 109:78]

Let the hearts of your brethren rejoice, and let the hearts of all my people rejoice, **who have, with their might, built this house to my name.** [D&C 110:6]

And again, verily I say unto you, how shall your washings be acceptable unto me, except ye **perform them in a house which you have built to my name?** . . .
And verily I say unto you, **let this house be built unto my name,** that I may reveal mine ordinances therein unto my people. . . .
And again, verily I say unto you, **I command you again to build a house to my name,** even in this place. [D&C 124:37, 40, 55; see also vv. 27, 39, 47, 51] [It is interesting that in this same section where there are seven references to a house (here meaning a temple) built unto His name, there are also three references to a house built "unto me" or "to me" (vv. 30, 31, 33).]

References to something built unto His name also appear in connection with the commandments to build the Nauvoo House (a boarding house) (see D&C 124:22, 24, 56), to **"build up cities unto my name"** (D&C 125:2), and to "build up" a particular "city **unto my name**" in Iowa (D&C 125:3). All of these commandments to build "unto my name" are easily understood as referring to building efforts to promote the overall work or plan of the Lord. Indeed, in one verse the Lord refers to men "do[ing] a work unto my name" (D&C 124:49).

These uses of "name" are clearly not references merely for identification, for in one of them the Lord specified that a name other than His was to be placed upon what was built ("and let the name of Zarahemla [Iowa] be named upon it" [D&C 125:3]). Also when the Lord desired that His name (identification) be put upon something to be built, He specifically commanded that:

> As pertaining to my boarding house which I have commanded you to build . . . , **let it be built unto my name, and let my name be named upon it.** [D&C 124:56]

This further confirms that building "to his name" is something beyond mere naming for identification.

PRAISE HIS NAME OR BLESS HIS NAME OR THOSE WHO COME IN HIS NAME

Scores of scriptures, especially in the Psalms, contain worshipful declarations blessing or praising the name of God or praising those who come in His name.

Perhaps some exclamations like "Praise His name" or "Bless His name" use the word *name* out of reluctance to make frequent or familiar use of the sacred name of God. But it is notable how many scriptures praise God by name and then separately praise His name. This separateness shows that in these instances "name" is not merely identification but carries an additional meaning. As we have seen, that additional meaning is to add praise to the work or plan God has established for the salvation and exaltation of His children. Illustrations follow:

Now therefore, our God, we thank thee, and **praise thy glorious name.** [1 Chr. 29:13]

PRAISE ye the LORD. Praise, O ye servants of the LORD, **praise the name of the LORD.** [Ps. 113:1]

PRAISE ye the LORD. **Praise ye the name of the LORD;** praise [him], O ye servants of the LORD. [Ps. 135:1]

Bring my soul out of prison, that I may **praise thy name:** the righteous shall compass me about; for thou shalt deal bountifully with me. [Ps. 142:7]

And ye shall eat in plenty, and be satisfied, and **praise the name of the LORD your God,** that hath dealt wondrously with you. [Joel 2:26]

I will boast of my God, for in his strength I can do all things; yea, behold, many mighty miracles we have wrought in this land, for which we will **praise his name forever.** [Alma 26:12]

And when they had all gone forth and had witnessed for themselves, they did cry out with one accord, saying:

Hosanna! **Blessed be the name of the Most High God!** And they did fall down at the feet of Jesus, and did worship him. [3 Ne. 11:16–17]

And the Lord God has spoken it; and **honor, power and glory be rendered to his holy name,** both now and ever. Amen. [D&C 20:36]

And the saints rejoiced in their redemption, and bowed the knee and acknowledged the Son of God as their Redeemer and Deliverer from death and the chains of hell.

Their countenances shone, and the radiance from the presence of the Lord rested upon them, and **they sang praises unto his holy name.** [D&C 138:23–24]

Another group of scriptures pronounce "blessed" those who come in the name of the Lord:

Blessed [be] he that cometh in the name of the LORD. [Ps. 118:26]

And the multitudes that went before, and that followed, cried, saying, Hosanna to the Son of David: **Blessed [is] he that cometh in the name of the Lord;** Hosanna in the highest. [Matt. 21:9]

On the next day much people that were come to the feast, when they heard that Jesus was coming to Jerusalem,

Took branches of palm trees, and went forth to meet him, and cried, Hosanna: **Blessed [is] the King of Israel that cometh in the name of the Lord.** [John 12:12–13]

HIS SERVANTS PROCLAIM HIS NAME OR BEAR HIS NAME OR SUFFER FOR HIS NAME

Scriptures that refer to preaching the gospel often do so in terms of "proclaiming" His name or "bearing" His name. Servants of the Lord are also described as suffering for His name (or namesake). These can all be understood as references to the Lord's plan—the message of gospel truths for which we may be called to suffer or sacrifice.

And in very deed for this [cause] have I raised thee up, for to shew [in] thee my power; and **that my name may be declared throughout all the earth.** [Ex. 9:16]

For I have purposed to take thee away out of Haran, and **to make of thee a minister to bear my name in a strange land** which I will give unto thy seed after thee for an everlasting possession, when they hearken to my voice. [Abr. 2:6]

And ye shall be **hated of all [men] for my name's sake:** but he that endureth to the end shall be saved. [Matt. 10:22]

Then shall they deliver you up to be afflicted, and shall kill you: and ye shall be **hated of all nations for my name's sake.** [Matt. 24:9]

Another use of the word *name* that can be read as signifying the gospel message or plan occurs in the great intercessory prayer, where Jesus prays to the Father:

I have **manifested thy name** unto the men which thou gavest me out of the world: thine they were, and thou gavest them me; and they have kept thy word. [John 17:6]

And now I am no more in the world, but these are in the world, and I come to thee. Holy Father, **keep through thine own name those whom thou hast given me,** that they may be one, as we [are].
While I was with them in the world, **I kept them in thy name:** those that thou gavest me I have kept, and none of them is lost, but the son of perdition; that the scripture might be fulfilled. [John 17:11–12]

And I have **declared unto them thy name,** and will declare [it]: that the love wherewith thou hast loved me may be in them, and I in them. [John 17:26]

Further examples of the frequent meaning of the word *name* to signify the message of the gospel are:

> But when they believed Philip **preaching the things concerning the kingdom of God, and the name of Jesus Christ,** they were baptized, both men and women. [Acts 8:12]

> For the scripture saith unto Pharaoh, Even for this same purpose have I raised thee up, that I might shew my power in thee, and **that my name might be declared throughout all the earth.** [Rom. 9:17]

> VERILY thus saith the Lord unto you my servant Thomas: I have heard thy prayers; and thine alms have come up as a memorial before me, in behalf of those, thy brethren, **who were chosen to bear testimony of my name and to send it abroad** among all nations, kindreds, tongues, and people, and ordained through the instrumentality of my servants. [D&C 112:1]

> Let thy heart be of good cheer before my face; and **thou shalt bear record of my name,** not only unto the Gentiles, but also unto the Jews; **and thou shalt send forth my word unto the ends of the earth.** . . .
> Let thy habitation be known in Zion, and remove not thy house; for I, the Lord, have **a great work for thee to do, in publishing my name among the children of men.** . . .

Wherefore, whithersoever they shall send you, go ye, and I will be with you; and **in whatsoever place ye shall proclaim my name** an effectual door shall be opened unto you, that they may receive my word. [D&C 112:4, 6, 19]

VERILY thus saith the Lord: It is wisdom in my servant David W. Patten, that he settle up all his business as soon as he possibly can, and make a disposition of his merchandise, that he may perform a mission unto me next spring, in company with others, even twelve including himself, **to testify of my name and bear glad tidings unto all the world.** [D&C 114:1]

I have seen your labor and toil in journeyings for my name. [D&C 126:2]

As a variation on this usage, numerous other scriptures refer to persecution or sacrifice for His name.

And when they had called the apostles, and beaten [them], they **commanded that they should not speak in the name of Jesus,** and let them go.

And they departed from the presence of the council, rejoicing that **they were counted worthy to suffer shame for his name.** [Acts 5:40–41]

But the Lord said unto him, Go thy way: for he is a chosen vessel unto me, **to bear my name before the Gentiles, and kings, and the children of Israel:**

For I will shew him **how great things he must suffer for my name's sake.** [Acts 9:15–16]

If ye be reproached for the name of Christ, happy [are ye]. [1 Peter 4:14]

And **all they who have given their lives for my name** shall be crowned. [D&C 101:15]

And **all they who suffer persecution for my name,** and endure in faith, though they are called to lay down their lives for my sake yet shall they partake of all this glory. [D&C 101:35]

HIS SERVANTS TAKE UPON THEM HIS NAME

The important covenant to take upon us His name, made at baptism and renewed weekly in partaking of the sacrament (discussed in chapter 6), goes well beyond the obvious significance of membership in a Church identified by the name of Jesus Christ. The words *take upon you the name of Christ* occur many times in the scriptures. Their frequent association with the words *having a determination to serve him to the end* or *endure to the end* reveals one of the most significant meanings of taking upon us the name of Christ: a willingness and a commitment to take upon us the work of the Savior and His kingdom. This includes testifying of Him, proclaiming His gospel, keeping His commandments, and accepting and fulfilling the callings and responsibilities necessary to do the work of His Church "to bring to pass the . . . eternal life of man." Examples follow:

> Wherefore, my beloved brethren, I know that if ye shall follow the Son . . . repenting of your sins, witnessing unto the Father that **ye are willing to take upon you the name of Christ, by baptism**—yea, by following your Lord and your Savior down into the water, according to his word . . . then shall ye receive the Holy Ghost. [2 Ne. 31:13]

> There is no other name given whereby salvation cometh; therefore, I would that ye should **take upon you the name of Christ,** all you that have entered into the covenant with God that ye should be obedient unto the end of your lives.
> And it shall come to pass that **whosoever doeth this** shall be found at the right hand of God, for he shall know the name by which he is called; for he **shall be called by the name of Christ.**
> And now it shall come to pass, that **whosoever shall not take upon him the name of Christ** must be called by some other name; therefore, he findeth himself on the left hand of God. [Mosiah 5:8–10]

> Have they not read the scriptures, which say **ye must take upon you the name of Christ,** which is my name? For **by this name** shall ye be called at the last day;

And **whoso taketh upon him my name,** and endureth to the end, the same shall be saved at the last day. [3 Ne. 27:5–6]

And none were received unto baptism save they **took upon them the name of Christ, having a determination to serve him to the end.** [Moro. 6:3]

And again, by way of commandment to the church concerning the manner of baptism—All those who humble themselves before God, and desire to be baptized, and come forth with broken hearts and contrite spirits, and witness before the church that they have truly repented of all their sins, and are willing to **take upon them the name of Jesus Christ, having a determination to serve him to the end,** and truly manifest by their works that they have received of the Spirit of Christ unto the remission of their sins, shall be received by baptism into his church. [D&C 20:37]

OTHER SCRIPTURES IN WHICH "NAME" SEEMS TO MEAN "WORK" OR "PLAN"

When we understand that a frequent scriptural meaning of "name" is "work" or "plan," it casts new light on some familiar scriptures. For example, the Lord's promise to be in the midst of us has new focus when we relate this to our gatherings *to promote His work or His plan:*

Verily, verily, I say unto you, as I said unto my disciples, **where two or three are gathered together in my name,** as touching one thing, behold, there will I be in the midst of them—even so am I in the midst of you. [D&C 6:32; see also Matt. 18:20]

As a further example, His oft-stated promises to give us whatever we ask in His name can be understood not just as referring to prayers offered in His name, but to *prayers whose content focuses on furthering His work or His plan.*

Verily, verily, I say unto you, **Whatsoever ye shall ask the Father in my name,** he will give [it] you. [John 16:23]

And **whatsoever ye shall ask the Father in my name,** which is right, believing that ye shall receive, behold it shall be given unto you. [3 Ne. 18:20; see also 3 Ne. 27:28, Moro. 7:26]

And if ye are purified and cleansed from all sin, **ye shall ask whatsoever you will in the name of Jesus and it shall be done.**
But know this, it shall be given you what you shall ask. [D&C 50:29–30]

Finally, the following wonderful promise seems to refer to those who are faithful in the work or plan of the Lord:

And **blessed is he that is found faithful unto my name at the last day,** for he shall be lifted up to dwell in the kingdom prepared for him from the foundation of the world. [Ether 4:19]

Chapter 5

NAME AS ESSENCE OR EXALTATION

$\mathcal{T}$here is one more meaning of the word *name,* as applied to Jesus Christ or God the Father, that incorporates all the other meanings and goes beyond. It comes from the meaning of the word *name* as signifying (or even embodying) the essence of the one named. In this meaning the scriptural words *name of the Lord* or *His name* or *My name* not only incorporate the ideas of His identity, His authority (priesthood), and His work, but also include the idea of *His essence, including His Godliness.* As we shall see, this interpretation is well supported in the scriptures themselves and in the commentary of scholarly authorities on one of the oldest meanings of the word *name.* When we read some scriptures to embody this meaning, we also find strong confirmation of the ancient Christian doctrine of deification and of the Latter-day Saint belief in exaltation.

NAME DESCRIBES ESSENCE

We begin this discussion of instances where the word *name* signifies the essence of the one named by recalling those numerous occasions where the Lord identifies Himself (or His prophets identify Him) by names that describe one of His qualities. In these scriptures, the name that signifies the Lord contributes to our understanding of His essence.

> And God spake unto Moses, saying: Behold, I am the Lord God Almighty, and **Endless is my name;** for I am without beginning of days or end of years; and is not this endless? [Moses 1:3]

> Behold, I am God; **Man of Holiness is my name; Man of Counsel is my name;** and **Endless and Eternal is my name,** also. [Moses 7:35]

In other scriptures the Lord described some of His qualities, preceded by the sacred words *I am.* This can be read as the equivalent of saying "my name is."

> Jesus said unto her, **I am the resurrection, and the life:** he that believeth in me, though he were dead, yet shall he live. [John 11:25]

> Jesus saith unto him, **I am the way, the truth, and the life:** no man cometh unto the Father, but by me. [John 14:6]

I am the light and the life of the world. I am Alpha and Omega, the beginning and the end. [3 Ne. 9:18]

Wherefore, I am in your midst, and **I am the good shepherd,** and the stone of Israel. He that buildeth upon this rock shall never fall. [D&C 50:44]

In still other scriptures, prophets identify the Lord by names that reveal some of His attributes:

For unto us a child is born, unto us a son is given: and the government shall be upon his shoulder: and **his name shall be called Wonderful, Counsellor, The mighty God, The everlasting Father, The Prince of Peace.** [Isa. 9:6]

And she shall bring forth a son, and thou shalt **call his name JESUS:** for he shall save his people from their sins.

Now all this was done, that it might be fulfilled which was spoken of the Lord by the prophet, saying,

Behold, a virgin shall be with child, and shall bring forth a son, and **they shall call his name Emmanuel, which being interpreted is, God with us.** [Matt. 1:21–23]

And now, my sons, I would that ye should look to **the great Mediator,** and hearken unto his great commandments. [2 Ne. 2:28]

For thy maker, thy husband, **the Lord of Hosts is his name; and thy Redeemer, the Holy One of Israel—the God of the whole earth** shall he be called. [3 Ne. 22:5; see also Isa. 54:5]

This revealing of the attributes of God has the important purpose of helping us to know God and thereby helping us toward eternal life (see John 17:3; discussed hereafter).

In the ancient world, a name represented the essence of the person named. Thus, a prominent Bible dictionary declares:

In biblical thought a name is not a mere label of identification; it is an expression of the essential nature of its bearer. A man's name reveals his character. . . . Hence to know the name of God is to know God as he has revealed himself. [*Interpreter's Dictionary,* 3:500–501]

Similarly, Rabbi Harold S. Kushner explains:

In ancient times, a name was more than an identifying label. Your name was your essence, what you were all about, your identity rather than just your identification. [Harold S. Kushner, *To Life!* (New York: Warner Books, 1994), 146]

After the Creation, the Lord brought every beast and fowl to Adam "to see what he would call them: and whatsoever Adam called every living creature, that was the name thereof" (Gen. 2:19). The dictionary explains, "Nothing exists unless it has a name. . . . Its essence is concentrated in its name" (*Interpreter's Dictionary*, 3:501). For this reason, in biblical thought a change of name signifies a change of nature or essence (see ibid, 2:408; 3:506). The dictionary observes:

> It could also be said soberly of anyone that his name *is* his very self. Thus, when a radical change in a person's character took place so that he became a new man, he was given a new name. [Ibid., 2:408]

Thus, a king receives a new name on his ascending the throne.

This understanding helps to explain the new names given to many key figures in the Bible at the time of an important change in their lives. Examples include Abraham (see Gen. 17:5), Sarah (see Gen. 17:15), Israel (see Gen. 32:28; 35:10), and Peter (see John 1:42). The idea that a name changes when a person's essence changes also helps to explain the scriptural teaching that a new name is given to all persons who come into the celestial kingdom (see D&C 130:11; see also Isa. 56:5, 62:2; Rev. 2:17, 3:12).

The most comprehensive biblical illustration of the significance of the word *name* as signifying the essence of the one named occurs in a conversation between the Lord and the prophet Moses. When the Lord spoke to Moses from the burning bush, He introduced Himself with these words: "I [am] the God of thy father, the God of Abraham, the God of Isaac, and the God of Jacob" (Ex. 3:6).

The scripture next reports the Lord's instructions to Moses about his assignment to deliver the children of Israel out of Pharaoh's captivity, and then records this significant exchange:

> And Moses said unto God, Behold, [when] I come unto the children of Israel, and shall say unto them, The God of your fathers hath sent me unto you; and they shall say to me, **What [is] his name?** what shall I say unto them?
>
> And God said unto Moses, **I AM THAT I AM:** and he said, Thus shalt thou say unto the children of Israel, I AM hath sent me unto you. [Ex. 3:13–14]

In English the words *I am* signify the state of being (the first person present tense of the verb *to be*). (In Latin, the verb of *being* is *esse*, which is the root source of *essence*.) Thus, when Moses asked to know the name of God, he was asking to know the essence or nature of God, and God answered in those same terms. The Bible dictionary quoted above concludes:

> The uses of the word "name" in the OT [Old Testament] are all related to the central conception of name as denoting essential being. This applies with regard to both man and God. . . .
>
> The name in the OT is the essence of personality, the expression of innermost being. [*Interpreter's Dictionary,* 3:501]

Similarly, the *Oxford Universal Dictionary* lists several secondary meanings of the word *name*, "chiefly of Biblical origin," including: (1) the name of God "as symbolizing the divine nature of power" and (2) the name of a person "as implying his individual characteristics" (*Oxford Universal Dictionary* [Oxford: Claredon Press, 3rd edition, revised, 1955], 1308). Each of these meanings came into the English language in time to influence the usage of the word *name* in the key English language translations of the Bible.

The fact that "God's self, his real person, is concentrated in his name" (*Interpreter's Dictionary*, 2:408) explains the sacredness of God's name in ancient thought. The Bible dictionary explains:

> Because the divine name discloses God's nature, it is laden with the authority, power, and holiness of God himself. This accounts for the great reverence for the name which is one of the distinctive features of Israel's faith. [Ibid.]

"In the post-exilic period (after 538 B.C.), however, the sacred name was withdrawn from popular usage for fear that it would be profaned" (*Interpreter's Dictionary*, 2:817). Such reactions seem to be attributable to the concept that a name signifies or even embodies the essence of the one named. The sacred beginning of the book of John ("IN the beginning was the Word, and the Word was with God, and the Word was God" [John 1:1]) also seems to be related to this subject.

This brief discussion has only scratched the surface of a subject that is holy and deep and little understood.

Several New Testament scriptures use the word *name* in ways that can be interpreted as a reference to the essence of the Lord.

Being made so much better than the angels, as **he hath by inheritance obtained a more excellent name than they.** [Heb. 1:4]

Wherefore **God also hath highly exalted him, and given him a name which is above every name:**

That at the name of Jesus every knee should bow, of things in heaven, and things in earth, and things under the earth;

And that every tongue should confess that Jesus Christ [is] Lord, to the glory of God the Father. [Philip. 2:9–11]

MORTAL DESTINATION AND THE DOCTRINE OF DEIFICATION

Understanding the word *name* as a reference to the essence of the one named opens the door to a fuller understanding of numerous scriptures concerning the glorious destination of the children of God. That goal identifies the ultimate purpose of the gospel plan and of The Church of Jesus Christ of Latter-day Saints. Here we touch upon the ancient doctrine of deification—man becoming a god (see, generally, Deification, Early Christian, *Encyclopedia of Mormonism* [New York: MacMillan, 1992], 1:369–70). A commonly taught doctrine in the first few centuries of the Christian era, deification was rejected and discredited by later scholars. Today it is a major point of difference between traditional Christians and Latter-day Saints.

Among the Bible scriptures relied upon to support the possibility of deification are John's references to Jesus having given mortals power to become "the sons of God" (John 1:12; 1 John 3:1) and his teaching that "when he shall appear, we shall be like him" (1 John 3:2). To the same effect is Peter's teaching that Jesus has "given unto us all things that pertain unto life and godliness" by which "great and precious promises" we "might be partakers of the divine nature" (2 Peter 1:3–4).

There are, of course, numerous confirming and even more direct references to deification in modern scriptures. Various chapters of the Book of Mormon and various sections of the Doctrine and Covenants affirm that through receiving Jesus Christ or through faith or belief on His name we can "become the sons of God" (3 Ne. 9:17; Moro. 7:26; D&C 11:30; 35:2), or "become my sons and my daughters" (Ether 3:14). One of the clearest such references is this:

> I came unto mine own, and mine own received me not; but unto as many as received me gave I power to do many miracles, and **to become the sons of God; and even unto them that believed on my name gave I power to obtain eternal life.** [D&C 45:8]

Section 76 of the Doctrine and Covenants, which has greater detail on this subject than any other published revelation, explains the meaning of "sons of God" when it describes those who will receive exaltation in the celestial kingdom as those "who have received of his fulness, and of his glory" (v. 56) and concludes, "Wherefore, as it is written, they are gods, even the sons of God" (v. 58).

THE PLAN OF SALVATION IS THE PROCESS BY WHICH THE CHILDREN OF GOD ATTAIN THE NAME (ESSENCE) OF CHRIST

Of equal significance to the above references to mortals becoming gods are the numerous teachings in modern scripture that describe the plan of salvation, which is the process by which this occurs.

Jesus Christ, the Redeemer and Savior of the world, is the essential life-giving source in the plan of salvation. His saving mission under this plan opens the door and points the way for the children of God to achieve their ultimate destination as sons and daughters of God—to become like Him. The plan of salvation is not only an expression of the authority and work of our Savior (see chapters 3 and 4). It is also a manifestation of His essence.

We began under that plan with a spirit-child relationship to God the Father. Through His plan and the work of His Only Begotten Son, our spirits were enabled to progress through mortality toward our eternal goal, which is to attain the exalted condition the Apostle Paul described as "unto a perfect man, unto the measure of the stature of the fulness of Christ" (Eph. 4:13). That description refers to a measure of the *essence* of Christ and His Father. As stated in modern revelation:

> I give unto you these sayings that you may understand and know how to worship, and know what you worship, that you may **come unto the Father in my name, and in due time receive of his fulness.** [D&C 93:19]

To "come unto the Father in [Christ's] name" is to come to the Father through compliance with the laws and ordinances and covenants specified in His plan. To receive of the fulness of the Father is to receive exaltation or eternal life.

The word *name* is threaded through the entire fabric of scriptural descriptions of the glorious plan of salvation, including its process and its intended result. The name of Jesus Christ was specified from the heavens (see Luke 1:31; Matt. 1:21). The word *name* sometimes means the work of salvation, which is the mission of the true Church of Jesus Christ. And the word *name* sometimes means the essence of Christ or the intended exaltation that is our destination and the result of the plan of salvation.

What could be more beautiful or more natural for God the Father than to desire and provide a means for His spirit children, who were created in His image, to become like He is? And what more natural means (more understandable to mortals) to enter upon that path than for His children to be born again—spiritually begotten—and to aspire to take upon them the name of their Creator? Taking that name upon us has obvious family implications, and it also serves to identify our destination as His children.

Many scriptures invoke the word *name* in connection with explaining our relationship to God the Father and His Son Jesus Christ and our eternal goal under their plan. Following are some that explain the plan by means of a vivid analogy to birth and to attaining the name (essence) of the Creator.

In his great valedictory teachings to his people, King Benjamin concluded with these words:

> And now, because of the covenant which ye have made ye shall be called the children of Christ, his sons, and his daughters, for behold, this day **he hath spiritually begotten you;** for ye say that **your hearts are changed through faith on his name;** therefore, **ye are born of him and have become his sons and his daughters.**
>
> And under this head ye are made free, and there is no other head whereby ye can be made free. There is **no other name given whereby salvation cometh;** therefore, I would that ye should **take upon you the name of Christ,** all you that have entered into the covenant with God that ye should be obedient unto the end of your lives.
>
> And it shall come to pass that whosoever doeth this shall be found at the right hand of God, for he shall **know the name by which he is called; for he**

shall be called by the name of Christ. [Mosiah 5:7–9]

Similar teachings were given by the Lord to the prophet Alma:

> Yea, blessed is this people who are **willing to bear my name; for in my name shall they be called;** and they are mine. . . .
>
> For behold, this is my church; whosoever is baptized shall be baptized unto repentance. And **whomsoever ye receive shall believe in my name;** and him will I freely forgive.
>
> For it is I that taketh upon me the sins of the world; for it is I that hath created them; and **it is I that granteth unto him that believeth unto the end a place at my right hand.**
>
> For behold, **in my name are they called;** and if they know me they shall come forth, and **shall have a place eternally at my right hand.** [Mosiah 26:18, 22–24]

In these scriptures we learn that those who are qualified by faith and repentance and compliance with the laws and ordinances of the gospel will have their sins borne by the Lord Jesus Christ. In spiritual and figurative terms they become the sons and daughters of Christ, heirs to His kingdom, with a place at His right hand eternally. These are they who will be called by His name and receive salvation/exaltation in the last day.

The resurrected Lord taught this same doctrine when He appeared to the Nephites.

Have they not read the scriptures, which say **ye must take upon you the name of Christ, which is my name? For by this name shall ye be called at the last day;**

And **whoso taketh upon him my name, and endureth to the end, the same shall be saved at the last day.** [3 Ne. 27:5–6]

This reference to taking upon us the name of Christ and being "saved at the last day" is a clear reference to exaltation, which means attaining the essence of Christ. Thus, in the concluding lecture on faith, the Prophet taught that "*salvation* [exaltation] *consists in the glory, authority, majesty, power and dominion which Jehovah possesses* and in nothing else; and no being can possess it but himself or one like him." (*Lectures on Faith,* 7:9) (Emphasis added.)

In other words, to be saved we must take upon us— attain to—the essence of Christ. This is the purpose and goal of His plan, including His atonement, His authority, and His commandments, under which we give obedience and service, receive ordinances, and make and keep covenants. The result of all of this is as Jesus explained:

Therefore **I would that ye should be perfect** even as I, or your Father who is in heaven is perfect. [3 Ne. 12:48; see also Matt. 5:48]

Therefore, **what manner of men ought ye to be?**
Verily I say unto you, **even as I am.** [3 Ne. 27:27]

These are references to the essence of Christ.

All of this fulfills the promises spoken to prophets,
ancient and modern.

Behold, I am he who was prepared from the foundation of the world to redeem my people. Behold, I
am Jesus Christ. I am the Father and the Son. **In me
shall all mankind have life, and that eternally, even
they who shall believe on my name; and they shall
become my sons and my daughters.** [Ether 3:14]

Behold, **Jesus Christ is the name which is given
of the Father, and there is none other name given
whereby man can be saved;**

Wherefore, **all men must take upon them the
name** which is given of the Father, for **in that name
shall they be called at the last day;**

Wherefore, **if they know not the name by which
they are called, they cannot have place in the kingdom of my Father.** [D&C 18:23–25]

Those who have lived so as to be able to take upon
them and be called by the name of Jesus Christ at the last
day are described in the great revelation recorded in the
ninety-third section of the Doctrine and Covenants. Here
the Savior declared that His teachings about the Father
and the Son were given

that you may understand and know how to worship, and know what you worship, **that you may come unto the Father in my name,** and in due time receive of his fulness.

For if you keep my commandments you shall receive of his fulness, and be glorified in me as I am in the Father. [D&C 93:19–20]

Here the Savior also bears record that "all those who are begotten through me are partakers of the glory of the same, and are the church of the Firstborn" (D&C 93:22).

In the revelation known as the Vision, the Lord gave this description of the church of the Firstborn:

They are they into whose hands the Father has given all things—. . . .

Wherefore, as it is written, they are gods, even the sons of God—. . . .

These shall dwell in the presence of God and his Christ forever and ever. [D&C 76:55, 58, 62]

The salvation/exaltation described in these revelations as the "fulness of the Father" is the ultimate significance of taking upon us the name of Jesus Christ. This is the teaching given by prophetic interpretation in the concluding lecture of *Lectures on Faith:*

These teachings of the Saviour *most clearly show unto us the nature of salvation,* and what he proposed unto the human family when he proposed to save them—that *he proposed to make them like unto himself, and he was like the Father, the great prototype of all saved beings; and for any portion of the human family to be assimilated into their likeness is to be saved.* [*Lectures on Faith*, 7:16] [Emphasis added.]

THE NAME (ESSENCE) OF GOD THE FATHER

Up to this point we have been discussing the "name" of our Savior, Jesus Christ. As we conclude this discussion of salvation/exaltation and eternal life, we rejoice in the illumination given to this subject by a rare scriptural reference to the "name" of God the Father. This was a principal subject in the intercessory prayer Jesus offered at the conclusion of His ministry. He prayed:

> And this is life eternal, that they might know thee the only true God, and Jesus Christ, whom thou hast sent. . . .
> **I have manifested thy name unto the men which thou gavest me** out of the world: thine they were, and thou gavest them me; and they have kept thy word. . . .
> And **I have declared unto them thy name,** and will declare [it]: that the love wherewith thou hast loved me may be in them, and I in them. [John 17:3, 6, 26]

In chapter 4 we suggested that the last two of these quoted verses referred to Jesus having taught His Apostles the gospel message or plan. But when we read these verses in the context of verse 3, which says that eternal life is to know God the Father, we see another important meaning, which is even recognized by a prominent Bible dictionary:

> Thus when Jesus is represented as saying "I have manifested thy name" (John 17:6, 26), the meaning is that his mission was to reveal the very character and purpose of God. [*Interpreter's Dictionary*, 2:208]

The implications of this dictionary statement go far beyond what its authors could have supposed. The first dictionary meaning of the word *character* is the attributes or traits that form the individual nature of a person. According to this meaning, when Jesus stated in His great intercessory prayer that He had "manifested" and "declared" to His Apostles the name of the Father (which the Bible dictionary defines as the "character and purpose of God"), He was referring to His having made them aware of the most fundamental essence in the whole universe—the essence of God the Father. The essence of this Heavenly Parent is the key to understanding the entire gospel plan, under which the children of God the Father can receive of His fulness and be exalted with Him. This key knowledge—the "name" or nature of the Father—is precisely what was lost in what Latter-day Saints call the Great Apostasy. All of the unique doctrines of what is called "Mormonism," which had to be restored in this dispensation of the fulness of times, are traceable to the fundamental understanding the Savior referred to as the "name" or essence of God the Father.

In his King Follett discourse, given at the culmination of his prophetic ministry, Joseph Smith asked "What kind of a being is God?" (*The Teachings of Joseph Smith,* ed. Larry E. Dahl and Donald Q. Cannon [Salt Lake City: Bookcraft, 1997], 295.) He soon asserted that "It is the first principle of the gospel to know for a certainty the character of God" (Ibid.). In truth, to understand the gospel plan we must begin with the truth about the nature of God (the "name" of God) and our relationship to Him. Everything else follows from that. When the religious world lost its understanding of the true nature of God, when they ceased to understand that He is our Father literally, and thereby reduced the fatherhood of God to an allegorical description, they lost sight of the purpose of the gospel plan.

As the Savior stated in His prayer, to know God the Father is to have eternal life. A knowledge of the true fatherhood of God is the crowning doctrine of Christ's ministry and of the gospel itself. It is the key to the true identity and destination of the children of God. It is the key to understanding the purposes of mortal life and the human family. It explains the glorious significance of the eternal family. This is why an understanding of the nature or essence (the "name") of God is the most important knowledge man can have.

Chapter 6

APPLICATIONS

*C*hapters one through five have discussed different meanings of the word *name* as used in various passages of scripture. This concluding chapter will apply these different meanings to three subjects of special interest in the gospel of Jesus Christ: (1) What does it mean when, in partaking of the sacrament, we witness to God that we are willing to take upon us the name of Jesus Christ? (2) What does it mean that an Apostle is a witness of the name of Jesus Christ in all the world? (3) Why do so many different scriptures refer to believing in or having faith in the "name of Jesus Christ" rather than in Jesus Christ Himself?

A. THE SACRAMENT COVENANT THAT WE ARE WILLING TO TAKE HIS NAME UPON US

Members of The Church of Jesus Christ of Latter-day Saints are commanded to partake of the sacrament each week (see D&C 59:9, 12). When the priest offers the scriptural prayer on the bread, he prays to God, the Eternal Father, that all who partake may "witness unto thee . . . that they are **willing to take upon them the name of thy Son**" (D&C 20:77; Moro. 4:3). This renews the covenant made in the waters of baptism (discussed in chapter 4) that we will **take upon us the name of Jesus Christ** and "serve him and keep his commandments" (Mosiah 18:10). In modern scriptures persons desiring to be baptized are required to witness before the Church "that they have truly repented of all their sins, and are **willing to take upon them the name of Jesus Christ,** having a determination to serve him to the end" (D&C 20:37; see also 2 Ne. 31:13; Moro. 6:3).

What does it mean when we covenant by baptism and by partaking of the sacrament that we are **"willing to take upon [us] the name of Jesus Christ?"** There are at least three meanings.

The first meaning concerns identification (discussed in chapter 2). We take upon us our Savior's name in this sense when we become members of the Church that bears His name. By His commandment, His Church is named The Church of Jesus Christ of Latter-day Saints (D&C 115:4). Similarly, we take upon us the name of Jesus Christ whenever we publicly proclaim our belief in Him. In this, we keep the modern commandment: **"Take upon you the name of Christ,** and speak the truth in soberness" (D&C 18:21). We also take upon us His name—His identity—whenever we act upon our faith in Him. Elder Jeffrey R. Holland explains this:

In as many ways as possible, both figuratively and literally, we try to take upon us his identity. We seek out his teachings and retell his miracles. We send latter-day witnesses, including prophets, apostles, and missionaries, around the world to declare his message. We call ourselves his children, and we testify that he is the only source of eternal life. ["Come Unto Me," *Ensign*, April 1998, 16]

A second significance of taking upon us the name of Christ applies the meaning of the name of God as the authority or work of God (discussed in chapters 3 and 4). By witnessing our willingness to take upon us the name of Jesus Christ, we signify our willingness to act in His authority and to do His work, which is to bring to pass the eternal life of man. By this means we covenant to accept callings in His Church and to be diligent in fulfilling the responsibilities of those callings. This meaning and this covenant cast new light on the third commandment, **"Thou shalt not take the name of the Lord thy God in vain"** (Ex. 20:7). More than a commandment against speaking the words of sacred names improperly (as by profanity), this is also a commandment not to be inactive in exercising His authority that has been conferred upon us or in carrying out that portion of His work that has been assigned to us.

The third meaning of our witnessed willingness to take upon us the name of Jesus Christ relies on the fact that what we witness is not that we *take* upon us His name but that we are *willing* to do so. This meaning must therefore relate to some future event or status that is not self-assumed, but depends on the authority or initiative of the Savior Himself. Only upon His action will we actually take His holy name upon us in this important sense.

What future event or status could this covenant contemplate? The implication of the discussion in chapter 5 suggests that this meaning of taking His name upon us concerns our relationship to our Savior and the incomprehensible blessings available to those who will eventually achieve what the Apostle Paul called "a perfect man [or woman], unto the measure of the stature of the fulness of Christ" (Eph. 4:13). According to this meaning, when we witness our *willingness* to take upon us the name of Jesus Christ, we are signifying our commitment to do all that we can to be counted among those whom He will choose to stand at His right hand and be called by His name (His essence) at the last day. In this sacred sense, our witness that we are "willing to take upon us the name of Jesus Christ" constitutes our declaration of candidacy for exaltation in the celestial kingdom. By this means we witness our determination to do all that we can to come unto Christ and receive the fulness of the Father, which is eternal life, "the greatest of all the gifts of God" (D&C 14:7).

In summary, we may think of the sacramental covenant to take upon us the name of Jesus Christ as comprising at least three meanings, each expressive of a different and ascending level of spiritual progress or maturity. First, we signify our willingness to be identified as a believer in Jesus Christ and as a member of the Church that bears His name and proclaims His gospel throughout the

world. Second, we signify our willingness to take upon us
our assigned measure of the authority and work of the
Savior to bring to pass the eternal life of the children of
God, including accepting and laboring diligently to fulfill
the responsibilities of our own callings in His kingdom.
Third, we witness our commitment to strive to qualify for
exaltation in the celestial kingdom.

B. APOSTLES AS WITNESSES OF HIS NAME

Apostles have two general types of duties, which they
exercise under the direction of the First Presidency: to
govern the Church and to witness to all the world. The
Seventies have duties that are similar but not identical.

As to governance, the Twelve are given distinct responsibilities, and the Seventy are to act under their direction:

> The Twelve are a Traveling Presiding High Coun-
> cil, *to officiate in the name of the Lord,* under the direction
> of the Presidency of the Church, agreeable to the in-
> stitution of heaven; to build up the church, and regu-
> late all the affairs of the same in all nations, first unto
> the Gentiles and secondly unto the Jews.
>
> The Seventy are *to act in the name of the Lord,* under
> the direction of the Twelve or the traveling high coun-
> cil, in building up the church and regulating all the af-
> fairs of the same in all nations, first unto the Gentiles
> and then to the Jews. [D&C 107:33–34] [Emphasis
> added.]

The hands-on work of building up the Church and regulating its affairs appears to be much the same for Apostles and Seventies, but a hierarchy of authority is clearly prescribed in the Twelve's "officiat[ing] . . . under the direction of the Presidency of the Church," and the Seventy's "act[ing] . . . under the direction of the Twelve."

As to witnessing, there are some differences in the following descriptions of the responsibilities given to the Apostles and the responsibilities given to the Seventies.

> The twelve traveling councilors are called to be the Twelve Apostles, or **special witnesses of the name of Christ in all the world**—thus differing from other officers in the church in the duties of their calling. [D&C 107:23]
>
> The Seventy are also called to preach the gospel, and to be *especial witnesses unto the Gentiles and in all the world*—thus differing from other officers in the church in the duties of their calling. [V. 25] [Emphasis added.]

Both Apostles and Seventies are "witnesses . . . in all the world." Beyond this, there are four differences in the descriptions of the callings of the Twelve Apostles and the callings of the Seventy.

> 1. The Seventy are described as "especial witnesses," whereas the Twelve are described as "special witnesses." If there is any substantive difference between an "especial" witness and a "special" witness, I have been unable to identify it.

2. The Seventy are called to "preach the gospel, and to be especial witnesses unto the Gentiles and in all the world." Witnesses of what? In this context, the meaning seems to be to preach the gospel of Jesus Christ and to witness of its truthfulness, duties also placed upon the Twelve.

3. The Seventy are specifically assigned to be "witnesses unto the Gentiles," which is apparently expressive of their special missionary responsibilities.

4. The Twelve Apostles are called to be "special **witnesses of the name of Christ** in all the world." What is the meaning of this important responsibility, which is unique to the Twelve?

In a revelation given in June 1829, the Lord described the future calling of Twelve Apostles:

And now, behold, there are others who are called to declare my gospel, both unto Gentile and unto Jew;

Yea, even twelve; and the Twelve shall be my disciples, and **they shall take upon them my name;** and the Twelve are they who shall desire to **take upon them my name with full purpose of heart.**

And if they desire to **take upon them my name with full purpose of heart,** they are called to go into all the world to preach my gospel unto every creature. [D&C 18:26–28]

In view of its two specific references to declaring or preaching the gospel, this earliest reference to the Apostles' taking upon them the name of Christ seems to be a reference to their taking upon them this preaching portion of the work of the Lord.

The Twelve Apostles' responsibilities to "take upon them my name" were given important elaboration in a revelation of August 1830, which introduces their relationship to priesthood keys. This is done in the context of the Lord's reference to a future time when He will partake of the sacrament with various prophets.

> And also with Peter, and James, and John, whom I have sent unto you, by whom I have ordained you and confirmed you to be **apostles, and especial witnesses of my name, and bear the keys of your ministry and of the same things which I revealed unto them;**
>
> **Unto whom I have committed the keys of my kingdom,** and a dispensation of the gospel for the last times; and for the fulness of times, in the which I will gather together in one all things, both which are in heaven, and which are on earth. [D&C 27:12–13]

Finally, the Apostle's unique duty of special witness is definitively stated in the March 1835 revelation quoted above.

> The twelve traveling councilors are called to be the Twelve Apostles, or **special witnesses of the name of Christ in all the world**—thus differing from other of-

ficers in the church in the duties of their calling.
[D&C 107:23] [Emphasis added.]

Most of the meanings of *name* discussed in chapters
3, 4, and 5 have obvious application to the verses quoted
above. First, an Apostle is a witness of the priesthood of
Jesus Christ (see chapter 3). He holds its keys, as stated in
the quoted verses in section 27 and in other revelations.
For example, in the July 1837 revelation about the duties
of the Quorum of the Twelve, the Lord declares that the
"power of this priesthood" and the "keys of the dispensation" are given to the Twelve and to the First Presidency
("your leaders") (D&C 112:30, 32). In addition, section
107 illustrates that meaning by several verses referring to
the Apostles' exercise of the keys of priesthood authority.
Verse 24 provides that the Apostles "form a quorum,
equal in authority and power" to the First Presidency.
Verse 33 declares that they "officiate in the name of the
Lord . . . to . . . regulate all the affairs" of the Church.
Verse 58 states that it is their duty "to ordain and set in
order all the other officers of the church." All three of
these provisions are references to priesthood authority,
and the Apostle has a special measure of that authority
and the keys to direct its exercise, as authorized, in all the
world.

Second, an Apostle is uniquely commissioned to serve
as a witness of the work of the Savior (see chapter 4): His
roles as Creator, Resurrector, Redeemer, Savior, and Judge,
the light and life of the world. This preeminent responsibility makes an Apostle responsible to witness of the great

atoning sacrifice of the Lord Jesus Christ and of His plan of salvation, with all of its doctrines, ordinances, commandments, covenants, and blessings.

Third, as discussed in chapter 5, the purpose of the plan of salvation is for each son or daughter of God to achieve his or her divine destination. As a witness of the name of Jesus Christ, an Apostle is the preeminent teacher and testifier of the ultimate purpose of the plan of salvation—for each of the sons and daughters of God to attain his or her divine potential of eternal life, or salvation/exaltation, which modern revelation calls the "fulness" of the Father.

The scriptures make clear that in all of their various duties the Twelve Apostles are to be directed by the First Presidency (see D&C 90:16; 107:22; 112:30; 124:126) and they are to be assisted by the Seventy, whom they are to call upon "instead of any others" (D&C 107:38). In a January 1841 revelation on the duties of various quorums, the Lord said of the quorum of seventies:

> Which quorum is instituted for traveling elders **to bear record of my name in all the world,** wherever the traveling high council, mine apostles, shall send them to prepare a way before my face. [D&C 124:139]

This quorum responsibility is obviously supportive of and subject to the Apostles' unique duty to be **"special witnesses of the name of Christ in all the world"** (D&C 107:23).

C. Belief in Christ vs. Belief in His Name

Why do so many different scriptures (discussed in chapter 4) refer to believing in or having faith in "the name of Jesus Christ" rather than in Jesus Christ?

At the outset we must stress that what is said here should not be understood as raising any question about the importance of "faith in the Lord Jesus Christ." That is the first principle of the gospel (see A of F 4), which precedes and undergirds all of the other principles discussed here. The question discussed at this point is, in view of the primacy of faith in the Lord Jesus Christ, why do some of the most important scriptures—including some concerning the remission of sins and salvation—refer to the *name* of Jesus Christ instead of to Jesus Christ Himself? Are we saved by Jesus Christ or by the name of Jesus Christ?

The totality of the scriptures and the teachings of modern prophets show that *we are saved by Jesus Christ through the name of Jesus Christ,* which means through the work and the plan of salvation mediated by Jesus Christ, most notably His resurrection and His atonement for our sins on the conditions He has prescribed.

It seems likely that a primary reason for the numerous important scriptural references to the *name* of our Savior instead of just to the Savior Himself is to emphasize the requirement of our doing something beyond merely believing in Christ. If the scriptural references to "the name of the Lord" or "His name" or "my name" are no more than a reference to the Lord Himself, then it would be easier to maintain that we are saved simply by belief in the Lord Himself. But if these frequent references to "name" mean believing in (and acting upon) *something in addition to the Lord Himself,* then these additional words are persuasive evidence that salvation requires something more than mere belief in Christ.

Numerous scriptures say we must have faith in or believe in His name. This seems to mean having faith in or believing in His work or His plan: His priesthood, His ordinances, His commandments, His covenants. When we understand that teaching, we have no doubt about how to resolve the familiar doctrinal dispute between those who believe we attain salvation merely by accepting Jesus Christ as our personal Savior ("salvation by grace") and those who believe we are obliged to keep the commandments, ordinances, and covenants prescribed in His plan (salvation by grace, "after all we can do" [2 Ne. 25:23]).

Jesus clearly taught the need for action, and one of the things He taught we must do to be saved is to be baptized. To the Nephites He taught this explicitly as a necessity in addition to belief in Him.

> And whoso believeth in me, *and is baptized,* the same shall be saved; and they are they who shall inherit the kingdom of God.
>
> And whoso believeth not in me, and is not baptized, shall be damned. [3 Ne. 11:33–34; see also John 3:3–5] [Emphasis added.]

The last sentence in this quote seems to imply that if we

really believe in Christ (in His name, His work) we *will* be baptized; damnation results from not believing and therefore not being baptized.

Jesus also taught the necessity of following Him, which involves taking up the cross of service to our fellowmen.

> Then said Jesus unto his disciples, If any [man] will come after me, let him deny himself, and take up his cross, and follow me. [Matt. 16:24]

To take up our cross and follow the Savior results in personal growth toward our divine destination.

To come unto Christ means to believe in, trust in, and accept (act upon) all of the teachings of His gospel, including the commandments, the ordinances, and the covenants. All of this is signified by the various meanings of the scriptural references to His name. Priesthood authority is required for the ordinances (e.g., baptism) He has prescribed. The work of the Lord, including His atonement and His resurrection, assures us immortality and opens the door for eternal life. The gospel plan, under which He has accomplished His work, also identifies the way we keep His commandments and our covenants. His essence is what we must *become* to achieve salvation/exaltation.

To come unto Christ is not satisfied by a mere confession or declaration of belief in Him. It means to *follow* Him in order to become as He is. As we seek to follow in His footsteps, we are reminded that He "received not of the fulness at first, but continued from grace to grace, until he received a fulness" (D&C 93:13). So it must be with us, His followers.

The idea that the words "my name" sometimes mean "my work" or "the plan of salvation" illuminates a puzzling scriptural teaching that appears in the fourteenth chapter of 3 Nephi and the seventh chapter of Matthew.

> Not every one that saith unto me, Lord, Lord, shall enter into the kingdom of heaven; but he that doeth the will of my Father who is in heaven.
>
> Many will say to me in that day: Lord, Lord, have we not **prophesied in thy name,** and **in thy name have cast out devils,** and **in thy name done many wonderful works?**
>
> And then will I profess unto them: I never knew you; depart from me, ye that work iniquity. [3 Ne. 14:21–23; see also Matt. 7:21–23]

Significantly, Joseph Smith's inspired translation gives the last verse as, "And then will I say, Ye never knew me; depart from me ye that work iniquity" (JST, Matt. 7:33).

Here the Savior taught a contrast. In the final judgment, many who have used the name of Christ to prophesy, to cast out devils, and to do "many wonderful works" are branded as workers of iniquity and are banished. In contrast, those who "[do] the will of my Father who is in heaven" will "enter into the kingdom of heaven." The difference is apparently between (1) those who do their own work in the name of Christ (anyone can speak His name or put His name upon anything), and (2) those who do the will (the work) of the Father.

The work of the Father is to bring to pass the eternal life of man (see Moses 1:39). This work is done (1) through the Church of His Son—simple things like laboring in our calling, however humble and hard—and (2) through our own families—bearing and raising children (as we are given the opportunity), however difficult and painful. In other words, it is not good enough to *use His name*, even in doing "wonderful works." To "enter into the kingdom of heaven" we must *take His name upon us* by doing the will (the work) of the Father.

This contrast between the effect of putting His name on our chosen work or being involved in glorifying or furthering His chosen work is further illustrated in Alma's teachings about those who hearken to the name called by the Good Shepherd:

> Yea, come unto me and bring forth works of righteousness, and ye shall not be hewn down and cast into the fire—
>
> For behold, the time is at hand that whosoever bringeth forth not good fruit, or whosoever doeth not the works of righteousness, the same have cause to wail and mourn.
>
> O ye workers of iniquity; ye that are puffed up in the vain things of the world, ye that have professed to have known the ways of righteousness nevertheless have gone astray, as sheep having no shepherd,

notwithstanding a shepherd hath called after you and is still calling after you, but ye will not hearken unto his voice!

Behold, I say unto you, that the good shepherd doth call you; yea, and **in his own name he doth call you, which is the name of Christ; and if ye will not hearken unto the voice of the good shepherd, to the name by which ye are called, behold, ye are not the sheep of the good shepherd.** [Alma 5:35–38]

The final verses of the next-to-last chapter of the book of John provide a fitting conclusion to this review of the meaning of the frequent additional references to belief in "His name" as showing that mere belief in Christ is insufficient. The setting of this chapter is the resurrected Lord's appearance to Mary Magdalene and the two separate appearances in which He showed Himself to the Apostles and bestowed the Holy Ghost upon them. The chapter concludes by repeating the teaching that we must have something beyond belief "that Jesus is the Christ."

And many other signs truly did Jesus in the presence of his disciples, which are not written in this book:

But these are written, that ye might believe that Jesus is the Christ, the Son of God; and that **believing ye might have life through his name.** [John 20:30–31]

The "life" referenced here is not just resurrection to immortality, for that is a merciful gift to all, irrespective of belief. The "life" offered here is eternal life, the ultimate goal of the children of God. This "life" comes "through his name." In this context, "his name" means His work and His plan of salvation, with all of its glorious provisions for the children of God.

Scripture Index

Old Testament

Genesis

2:19	2
2:19	47
4:26	1
17:5	2
17:5	47
17:15	47
32:28	47
35:10	47

Exodus

3:6	47
3:13–14	48
9:16	33
20:7	2
20:7	13
20:7	65
23:21	17

Leviticus

24:16	3

1 Samuel

16:13	11
17:45	11
25:5, 9	16

1 Kings

5:5	28
8:20	28
9:3	15
18:24	8

1 Chronicles

16:34–35	6
22:17, 19	28
22:19	1
29:13	31

New Testament

BOOK OF MORMON

DOCTRINE AND COVENANTS

PEARL OF GREAT PRICE

SUBJECT INDEX

learns of God's essence,
44, 47, 48
"my work and my glory,"
19

— N —

Name(s), changing of, 2, 47
of God in vain, 2–3, 13,
18
importance of, 2
often shows allegiance, 2
Name (term), as an authorized agent, 15–18
dictionary meaning of, 5,
48–49
as essence, 43–50, 57–61
as exaltation, 50–61, 66,
67, 75, 77, 79
as identification, 5–8
to identify Lord's Church,
20–21, 64
as priesthood authority or
power, 9–18, 65, 67
as salvation, 22–27, 53,
73–74
as Savior's atonement,
19, 22–23, 56, 71–72,
75
to signify gospel message,
33–36
uses of, 1–3

as work or plan, 19–41,
65, 71–72
Nauvoo House, 29
Nephi, did miracles in the
name of Jesus Christ, 10
Nephites, 2, 20, 56
New names, 2, 47
New Testament, *name* as
essence in the, 50

— O —

Obedience, 56
Ordinances, 10, 14, 17, 25,
53, 55, 56, 74, 75

— P —

Palm branches, 33
Patten, David W., 36
Paul, "unto a perfect man,"
52–53, 66
Persecution, 36–37
Peter (Apostle), did miracles
in the name of Jesus
Christ, 10–11
on divine nature, 51
new name of, 47
Pharaoh, 35, 48
Philip, 35
Plan of salvation, 19,
52–59, 72, 74

Power, *name* as, 9–18
Praising the name of Jesus
    Christ, 30–33
Prayer, acting in the name
    of the Lord through, 18
    as calling upon His name,
    1
    in the name of Jesus
    Christ, 40
Priesthood, keys, 15, 70,
    71
    name as, 9–18
    ordinances in the name of
    Jesus Christ, 10, 17–18
Priests, 64
Profanity, 65
Prophets, spoke in the name
    of the Lord, 11
Psalms, 30

— Q —

Quorum of the Twelve
    Apostles. *See* Apostles

— R —

Redemption, 22–23, 32
Repentance, 55
Representatives of Jesus
    Christ, 15–18
Resurrection, 14, 19, 75

Revelation, and believing on
    His name, 14
Reverence, 5
Rigdon, Sidney, 17

— S —

Sacrament, Christ will par-
    take of, 70
    and taking the name of
    Christ, 2, 37, 63–67
Sacrifice, personal, 36–37
Sacrifices, animal, in the
    name of Jesus Christ, 10
Salvation, comes through
    His name, 1, 23–27,
    31, 53, 73–74
    by grace, 74
Samuel, 11
Sarah, 47
Satan, commanded in the
    name of Jesus Christ,
    10
Service, 75
Seventies, and Apostles,
    67–70
    bear record of His name,
    2, 67–70
    use authority of His
    name, 9
Sins, remission of through
    His name, 1